MORE SUPER · SIMPLE SCIENCE ·

SCIENCE EXPERIMENTS WITH

LIQUID

A Division of ABDO
ABDO
Publishing Company

BY ALEX KUSKOWSKI   Consulting Editor, Diane Craig, M.A./Reading Specialist

visit us at www.abdopublishing.com

Published by ABDO Publishing Company, a division of ABDO, P.O. Box 398166, Minneapolis, Minnesota 55439. Copyright © 2014 by Abdo Consulting Group, Inc. International copyrights reserved in all countries. No part of this book may be reproduced in any form without written permission from the publisher. Super SandCastle™ is a trademark and logo of ABDO Publishing Company.

Printed in the United States of America, North Mankato, Minnesota
062013
112013

PRINTED ON RECYCLED PAPER

Editor: Liz Salzmann
Content Developer: Alex Kuskowski
Cover and Interior Design and Production: Mighty Media, Inc.
Photo Credits: Aaron DeYoe, Shutterstock

The following manufacturers/names appearing in this book are trademarks: Argo®, Arm & Hammer®, Gedney®, Karo®, Learning Resources®, Morton®, Pyrex®, Sharpie®, SoilMoist™, Sunbeam®, Ping-Pong®

Library of Congress Cataloging-in-Publication Data
Kuskowski, Alex.
  Science Experiments with liquid / by Alex Kuskowski ; consulting editor, Diane Craig.
     p. cm. -- (More super simple science)
  Audience: 005-010.
  ISBN 978-1-61783-852-1
  1. Liquids--Experiments--Juvenile literature. 2. Science--Methodology--Juvenile literature. I. Craig, Diane. II. Title.
  QC145.24.K87 2014
  530.42078--dc23
                          2012049953

Super SandCastle™ books are created by a team of professional educators, reading specialists, and content developers around five essential components—phonemic awareness, phonics, vocabulary, text comprehension, and fluency—to assist young readers as they develop reading skills and strategies and increase their general knowledge. All books are written, reviewed, and leveled for guided reading, early reading intervention, and Accelerated Reader® programs for use in shared, guided, and independent reading and writing activities to support a balanced approach to literacy instruction.

TO ADULT HELPERS

Learning about science is fun and simple to do. There are just a few things to remember to keep kids safe. Some activities in this book recommend adult supervision. Be sure to review the activities before starting, and be ready to assist your budding scientist when necessary.

KEY SYMBOL

Look for this symbol in this book.

HOT!
You will be working with something hot. Get help!

TABLE OF CONTENTS

SUPER SIMPLE SCIENCE

You can be a scientist! It's super simple. Science is all around you. Learning about the world around you is part of the fun of science. Science is in your house, your backyard, and on the playground.

Find science in lemons and milk. Look for science in butter or blackberries. Try the activities in this book. You'll never know where to find science unless you look!

SCIENCE WITH LIQUID

Learn about science with liquid. A liquid is a type of matter that is wet and flows easily. In this book you will see how liquids can help you learn about science.

WORK LIKE A SCIENTIST

Scientists have a special way of working. It is a series of steps called the Scientific Method. Follow the steps to work like a scientist.

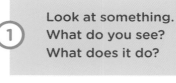

1. Look at something. What do you see? What does it do?

2. Think of a question about the thing you are watching. What is it like? Why is it like that? How did it get that way?

3. Think of a possible answer to the question.

4. Do a test to find out if you are right. Write down what happened.

5. Think about it. Were you right? Why or why not?

KEEP TRACK

There's another way to be just like a scientist. Scientists make notes about everything they do. So get a notebook. When you do an experiment, write down what happens in each step. It's super simple!

WHAT YOU WILL NEED

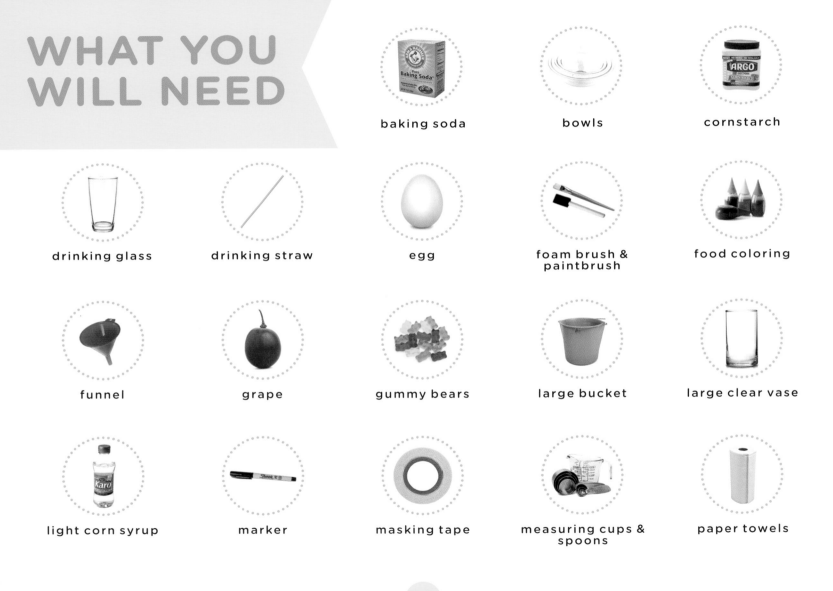

baking soda

bowls

cornstarch

drinking glass

drinking straw

egg

foam brush & paintbrush

food coloring

funnel

grape

gummy bears

large bucket

large clear vase

light corn syrup

marker

masking tape

measuring cups & spoons

paper towels

paperclips

pennies

pie pan

Ping-Pong ball

plastic bead,
button, & bottle
cap

plastic comb

prune juice

rubbing alcohol

ruler

scissors

spoons

styrofoam &
plastic cups

table salt & rock
salt

thermometer

tongs

toothpicks

vegetable oil

vinegar

water
(seltzer bottles,
distilled)

water storing
crystals

01

WONDERFUL WATER WHISTLE

WHAT YOU WILL NEED

drinking straw

ruler

marker

scissors

plastic cup

water

DIRECTIONS

① Make a mark 2½ inches (6.3 cm) from one end of the straw.

② Cut almost all the way through the straw at the mark. Leave a small piece uncut. Bend the straw at the cut. Don't break it.

③ Fill the cup with water. Put the long end of the straw in the water.

4 Keep the straw bent sideways. Blow through the short end of the straw. Move the straw up and down in the water. What happens?

WHAT'S GOING ON?

Blowing air across the long end of the straw makes a whistling sound. Lowering the straw reduces the space in the straw above the water. The whistle gets higher. Raising the straw makes the whistle lower.

02 OUT-OF-SIGHT SECRET MESSAGE

WHAT YOU WILL NEED

¼ cup baking soda

¼ cup water

measuring cups

2 small bowls

spoon

3 cups prune juice

paintbrush

paper

foam brush

DIRECTIONS

1. Mix the baking soda and water in one bowl. Put the prune juice in the second bowl.

2. Dip the paintbrush in the baking soda mixture. Write a message on the paper. Let it dry.

3. Dip the foam brush in the prune juice. Spread the juice over the paper.

4. Repeat step 3 until the message appears!

WHAT'S GOING ON?

Prune juice is an **acid**. It has chemicals that change color when mixed with a **base**. Baking soda is a base. The writing is revealed when the juice touches the baking soda on the paper.

03 SHRINK & GROW GUMMY BEARS

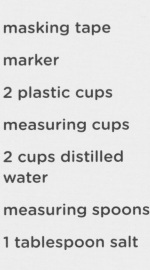

WHAT YOU WILL NEED

masking tape

marker

2 plastic cups

measuring cups

2 cups distilled water

measuring spoons

1 tablespoon salt

spoon

2 gummy bears

DIRECTIONS

1. Use tape to label the cups "water" and "salt water." Put 1 cup distilled water in each cup.

2. Add the salt to the cup labeled "salt water." Stir it with a spoon.

3. Put a gummy bear in each cup. Let it sit for 24 hours.

4. Take the gummy bears out of the cups. Compare the sizes.

WHAT'S GOING ON?

The gummy bear in the fresh water **absorbed** the liquid. So it gets bigger. The salt water takes liquid from the gummy bear. So the gummy gets smaller.

04 COLORFUL WATER CRYSTALS

WHAT YOU WILL NEED

5 plastic cups

water

food coloring

water storing crystals (found at gardening stores)

measuring spoons

large clear vase

DIRECTIONS

① Fill each cup with water. Add 4 drops of food coloring to each cup. Make each one a different color.

② Pour 1 teaspoon of water storing crystals in each cup. Wait 1 hour.

3 Feel inside the glasses. What has changed?

④ Pour each cup into the vase one at a time. Let it sit for 24 hours. What has changed?

WHAT'S GOING ON?

Water storing crystals are made of a special plastic that **absorbs** water. When the crystals touch each other, some lose water. Others re-absorb it. The colors blend.

05 CLEANING UP COPPER

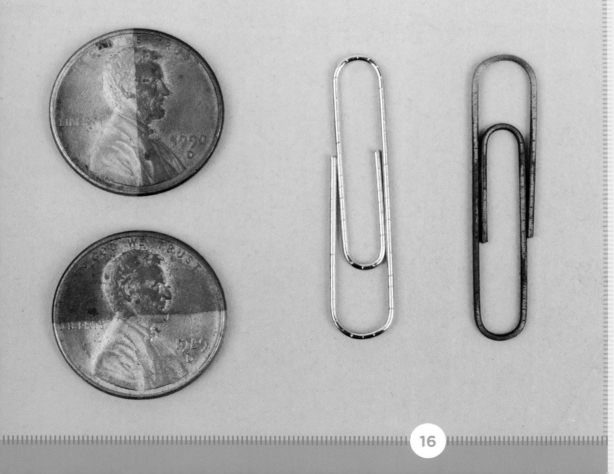

WHAT YOU WILL NEED

measuring cups & spoons

2 small bowls

¼ cup water

¼ cup vinegar

1 teaspoon salt

spoon

11 pennies

paper towel

2 paperclips

DIRECTIONS PART 1

1. Put the water in one bowl. Put the vinegar in the other bowl. Add the salt to the vinegar. Stir.

2. Put ten pennies in the bowl of vinegar. Wait 5 minutes. Dip half of the last penny in the vinegar. Hold it there for 30 seconds. Take it out. What's different?

3. Take out five pennies. Rinse them in the water. Dry them with a paper towel.

4. Take out the other five pennies. Put them on a paper towel. Do not dry them. Wait 30 minutes. What's different now?

WHAT'S GOING ON?

Over time, air makes copper dull. The vinegar mixture makes them shiny again. When left to dry, the vinegar **reacts** with the air. The pennies become dull again.

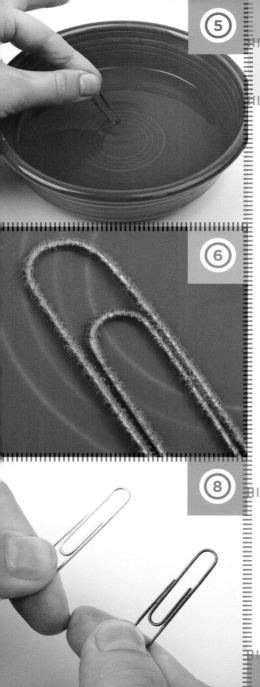

DIRECTIONS PART 2

⑤ Put one of the paperclips in the vinegar mixture from Part 1.

⑥ Let it sit for 1 hour. Look to see bubbles covering the paperclip.

7 Let it sit for 1 more hour. Take out the paperclip. Dry it off.

⑧ Compare the paperclip that was in the vinegar with the other paperclip.

WHAT'S GOING ON?

The vinegar mixture took the coating off the paperclip. Some copper from the pennies was left in the vinegar mixture. The copper stuck to the paperclip.

06

FLOATING ON LIQUID RAINBOWS

WHAT YOU WILL NEED

measuring cups

½ cup light corn syrup

½ cup water

½ cup vegetable oil

½ cup rubbing alcohol

4 plastic cups

clear drinking glass

food coloring

3 spoons

funnel

plastic button

grape

plastic bead

bottle cap

Ping-Pong ball

DIRECTIONS PART 1

① Put the corn syrup, water, vegetable oil, and rubbing alcohol in different cups.

② Put a drop of blue food coloring in the corn syrup. Put a drop of green food coloring in the water. Put a drop of red food coloring in the rubbing alcohol. Stir each glass with a different spoon.

③ Use the funnel to slowly pour the corn syrup into the clear drinking glass. Don't let the liquid touch the sides. Wash the funnel.

WHAT'S GOING ON?

The liquids have different **densities**. Density affects how heavy a liquid is. Corn syrup is the densest. It sinks to the bottom. Rubbing alcohol is the least dense. It floats to the top.

DIRECTIONS PART 2

4 Repeat step 3 with the water, vegetable oil, and rubbing alcohol. What do the liquids do?

5 Drop the button into the glass of layered liquids.

6 Drop the grape into the glass.

7 Drop the bead and the bottle cap into the glass.

8 Drop the Ping-Pong ball into the glass.

WHAT'S GOING ON?

Like the liquids, objects have different **densities**. They all float in order of density. For example, the grape is denser than water. But it is less dense than corn syrup. So it stays between them.

07 FANTASTIC FAST FREEZE

WHAT YOU WILL NEED

sealed plastic bottles of seltzer water

large bucket

ice

rock salt

thermometer

DIRECTIONS

1   Put the bottles of seltzer water in the refrigerator.

2   Wait 2 hours. Then fill the bucket with ice. Cover the ice with a layer of rock salt. Put the bottles in the bucket. Push them down so the ice covers them.

3   Put the thermometer in the ice near a bottle. Watch the thermometer. Wait until the temperature is at 17 degrees for 15 minutes.

4   Slowly take a bottle out of the ice. Open it. Repeat with other bottles. What happens?

WHAT'S GOING ON?

Seltzer water has **carbon dioxide** in it. The carbon dioxide makes it freeze more slowly. When you open the bottle, carbon dioxide escapes. The chilled water freezes as soon as the carbon dioxide is gone.

(08) EGG-CELLENT RUBBER EGG

WHAT YOU WILL NEED

egg

clear drinking glass

2 cups vinegar

measuring cups

water

bowl

DIRECTIONS

1. Put the egg and 1 cup vinegar in the glass. Let it sit for 24 hours. Bubbles will form on the shell.

2. Pour the vinegar out slowly. Add a new cup of vinegar. Let it sit for 7 days.

3. Pour the vinegar out. Fill the bowl with water. Rinse the egg in the bowl.

4. Poke the egg. What happens? Drop the egg 1 inch (2.5 cm) onto a flat surface. Drop the egg 2 inches (5 cm). What happens?

WHAT'S GOING ON?

The vinegar **reacts** with the egg's shell and causes bubbles. They remove part of the shell. What is left is soft and rubbery.

09 MYSTERIOUS GREEN SLIME

WHAT YOU WILL NEED

measuring cups

1½ cups cornstarch

1 cup water

bowl

spoon

green food coloring

DIRECTIONS

1. Put ½ cup cornstarch and ½ cup water in the bowl. Stir it with a spoon. Add the rest of the cornstarch and water a ½ cup at a time.

2. Add a few drops of green food coloring.

3. Stir with a spoon for 5 minutes. Then mix it with your hands.

4. Play with the mixture. Stretch it. Drop it. Watch it flow.

WHAT'S GOING ON?

The starch water is a **polymer**. Its **molecules** link together in a special way. They make a slime that can change its form. It can be a liquid or a solid.

10 WONDROUS RISING WATERS

WHAT YOU WILL NEED

plastic cup

water

food coloring

pie pan

large bowl

drinking glass

tongs

DIRECTIONS

1. Fill the plastic cup with water. Add 3 drops of food coloring.

2. Pour the water into the pie pan.

3. Fill the large bowl with very hot water. Put the glass in the hot water. Wait 30 seconds.

4. Use tongs to take the glass out of the hot water. Place it upside down in the pie pan. Watch for 5 minutes. What happens?

WHAT'S GOING ON?

Hot air takes up more space than cold air. When the hot air in the glass cooled, it created space inside the glass. Water was sucked in from outside the glass to fill the space.

11 SIMPLE STATIC WATER BEND

WHAT YOU WILL NEED

Styrofoam cup

toothpick

bowl

water

food coloring

plastic comb

DIRECTIONS

1. Poke a hole in the bottom of the cup with a toothpick. Leave the toothpick in the hole.

2. Hold the cup directly above the bowl. Fill the cup with water. Add a few drops of food coloring.

3. Run the comb through your hair a few times.

4. Take the toothpick out. Hold the points of the comb close to the stream of water. Be careful to not touch the water.

WHAT'S GOING ON?

Static electricity collects on the comb when you comb your hair. The water has static too. The static in the water is pulled toward the static on the comb. The stream of water bends toward the comb.

CONCLUSION

You just found out that science can be super simple! And you did it using liquids. Keep your thinking cap on! What other experiments can you do with liquids?

GLOSSARY

absorb – to soak up or take in.

acid – a type of chemical that reacts when mixed with a base.

base – a type of chemical that reacts when mixed with an acid.

carbon dioxide – a gas used to make fizzy, bubbly drinks.

molecule – a group of two or more atoms that make up the smallest piece of something.

polymer – a chemical compound that is made up by chains of smaller molecules that are all the same.

react – to change when mixed with another chemical.

static electricity – electricity that is on an object, often created by rubbing the object against something.